**Put Beginning Readers on the Right Track with
ALL ABOARD READING™**

The All Aboard Reading series is especially designed for beginning readers. Written by noted authors and illustrated in full color, these are books that children really *want* to read—books to excite their imagination, expand their interests, make them laugh, and support their feelings. With fiction and nonfiction stories that are high interest and curriculum-related, All Aboard Reading books offer something for every young reader. And with four different reading levels, the All Aboard Reading series lets you choose which books are most appropriate for your children and their growing abilities.

Picture Readers
Picture Readers have super-simple texts, with many nouns appearing as rebus pictures. At the end of each book are 24 flash cards—on one side is a rebus picture; on the other side is the written-out word.

Station Stop 1
Station Stop 1 books are best for children who have just begun to read. Simple words and big type make these early reading experiences more comfortable. Picture clues help children to figure out the words on the page. Lots of repetition throughout the text helps children to predict the next word or phrase—an essential step in developing word recognition.

Station Stop 2
Station Stop 2 books are written specifically for children who are reading with help. Short sentences make it easier for early readers to understand what they are reading. Simple plots and simple dialogue help children with reading comprehension.

Station Stop 3
Station Stop 3 books are perfect for children who are reading alone. With longer text and harder words, these books appeal to children who have mastered basic reading skills. More complex stories captivate children who are ready for more challenging books.

In addition to All Aboard Reading books, look for All Aboard Math Readers™ (fiction stories that teach math concepts children are learning in school); All Aboard Science Readers™ (nonfiction books that explore the most fascinating science topics in age-appropriate language); All Aboard Poetry Readers™ (funny, rhyming poems for readers of all levels); and All Aboard Mystery Readers™ (puzzling tales where children piece together evidence with the characters).

All Aboard for happy reading!

GROSSET & DUNLAP
Published by the Penguin Group
Penguin Group (USA) Inc., 375 Hudson Street, New York, New York 10014, USA
Penguin Group (Canada), 90 Eglinton Avenue East, Suite 700, Toronto, Ontario M4P 2Y3,
Canada (a division of Pearson Penguin Canada Inc.)
Penguin Books Ltd., 80 Strand, London WC2R 0RL, England
Penguin Group Ireland, 25 St. Stephen's Green, Dublin 2, Ireland
(a division of Penguin Books Ltd.)
Penguin Group (Australia), 250 Camberwell Road, Camberwell,
Victoria 3124, Australia (a division of Pearson Australia Group Pty. Ltd.)
Penguin Books India Pvt. Ltd., 11 Community Centre,
Panchsheel Park, New Delhi—110 017, India
Penguin Group (NZ), 67 Apollo Drive, Rosedale,
North Shore 0632, New Zealand (a division of Pearson New Zealand Ltd.)
Penguin Books (South Africa) (Pty.) Ltd., 24 Sturdee Avenue,
Rosebank, Johannesburg 2196, South Africa

Penguin Books Ltd., Registered Offices: 80 Strand, London WC2R 0RL, England

Photo credits: cover: © UpperCut Images Photography/Veer Inc.; page 3: © David Pedre/
iStockphoto/iStock International Inc.; pages 8–9: © fotoVoyager/iStockphoto/iStock
International Inc.; pages 12–13: © O. Louis Mazzatenta/National Geographic Stock;
pages 14–15: © Image Source Photography/Veer Inc.; page 19: © Ilya Terentyev/
iStockphoto/iStock International Inc.; page 29: © KingWu/iStockphoto/iStock International
Inc.; page 30: © Zhou kang/Imaginechina; page 31: © Hung Chung Chih 2010 Used under
license from Shutterstock.com; page 32: © Alan Tobey/iStockphoto/iStock International Inc.;
page 33: © O. Louis Mazzatenta/National Geographic Stock; pages 36–37: © Holger Mette/
iStockphoto/iStock International Inc., (lower left) © ximena yepes/iStockphoto/iStock
International Inc., (upper right) © Ben Jeayes/iStockphoto/iStock International Inc.;
pages 39–41: © O. Louis Mazzatenta/National Geographic Stock; page 42: © Doug Stern/
National Geographic Stock; pages 43–45: © O. Louis Mazzatenta/National Geographic
Stock; pages 46–47: © Huan wei/Imaginechina; page 48: © O. Louis Mazzatenta/National
Geographic Stock.

Library of Congress Control Number: 2010026578

ISBN 978-0-448-45580-8   10 9 8 7 6 5 4 3 2 1

HIDDEN ARMY
Clay Soldiers of Ancient China

by Jane O'Connor
illustrated by Erfian Asafat and Caravan Studio
and with photographs

Grosset & Dunlap
An Imprint of Penguin Group (USA) Inc.

Chapter One

Silent Soldiers

It is 210 BC and the moment before battle. The Chinese emperor's army is ready to charge. The soldiers—thousands of them—are lined up, row after row, as far as the eye can see. They are armed with crossbows, battle-axes, swords, and daggers.

The archers are in the front rows. They are closest to the enemy and make easy targets. Yet they do not have on helmets or wear armor to protect themselves. Armor is only for important officers whose lives are more valued.

Farther back in line, a general stands in a chariot. He is about to beat his drum. This will be the signal to attack! But the signal never comes. The army will never attack.

The soldiers are not real. They are the size of real soldiers. But they are made of terra-cotta, a strong kind of clay.

The soldiers are more than 2,000 years old. For almost all of that time, they lay hidden about 20 feet underground in China. (The map below shows the spot where the army was buried.) Until 1974, nobody knew the army was there.

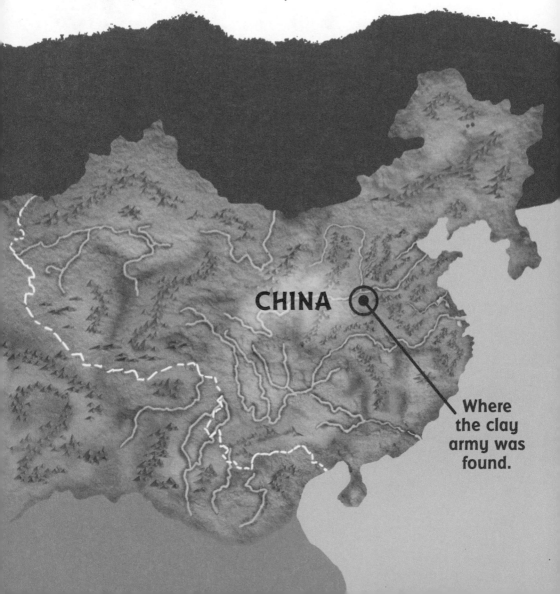

CHINA

Where the clay army was found.

Then one spring day, some farmers were digging a well. Their shovels hit something hard. Was it a rock?

No.

To their surprise, they dug up the clay head of a man. It looked very old. Who put it there and why? The farmers had no idea.

Soon archaeologists (say: are-key-OL-oh-jists) came to take a look at the head. Archaeologists study very old objects so they can learn about the past and the way people lived long ago.

The archaeologists hoped to find the rest of the clay man. They ended up finding much more than that.

Since 1974, more than 2,000 soldiers have been dug up. There may be as many as 6,000 more. Workers must assemble the soldiers from many small pieces of clay. It is like working on a 3-D jigsaw puzzle.

Besides the clay army, other things have also been unearthed, like bronze geese, clay acrobats, and two bronze war chariots. Who buried all these treasures—and why? It is an amazing story!

Chapter Two

The First Emperor

Today, China is the fourth-largest country in the world, with a population of more than one billion people. Beijing, seen here, is the capital of China and home to over 22 million people.

But before 221 BC, there was no such country as China. Instead, the area had seven different kingdoms. They were all at war with one another. The strongest kingdom was called Qin (say: CHIN—which sounds similar to the word *China*). The king of Qin was only 13 years old when he came into power, but he grew to be a fierce ruler.

The king of Qin conquered the other kingdoms one by one. By the time he was 37, he ruled over a huge empire.

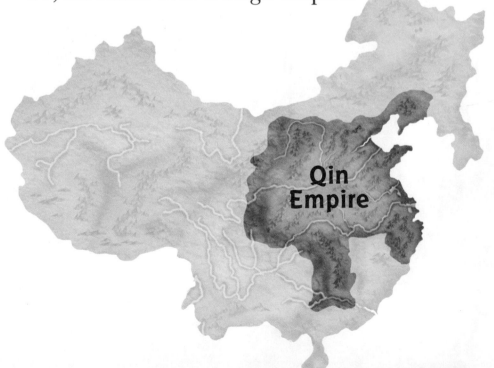

Qin Empire

The Qin king now made everyone call him First Emperor and Almighty of the Universe. That sounded important enough!

Indeed, the emperor did do some great things. He was afraid of enemies outside his empire, so he built the first Great Wall of China to protect his lands.

It was almost 3,000 miles long. (He didn't start the wall from scratch: Existing walls were connected and then extended.)

The emperor also feared enemies inside his empire. Many people were loyal to their old kingdoms. The emperor put a stop to that. He made everyone speak and write the same language. He made everyone use the same money and system of weights. He forced people to be part of his new empire.

There was one enemy, however, that the emperor could not defeat. That enemy was death.

More than anything, the emperor wanted to live forever.

According to legend, there were mysterious islands off the coast of China. They were called the Eastern Islands. The people there knew how to make a magic potion. It kept them alive forever.

Many times the emperor sent search parties out to sea. But they never found the Eastern Islands or the magic potion.

With no way to stop death, the
emperor did the next best thing. He had
700,000 workers build him a magnificent
tomb. He was only 13 years old when the
work began. The tomb was in the shape
of a pyramid. It was even bigger than the
Great Pyramid in Egypt.

The ceiling of the main room was
supposedly covered with jewels. It was
meant to look like the sky. Below it were
rivers in the shapes of the Yellow River and
the Yangtze River. The rivers were made of

mercury, a poisonous liquid. They flowed past models of the emperor's palaces.

The ancient Chinese believed that a person's spirit lived on after death. In fact, they thought that life after death was a lot like life on earth. So the emperor filled his tomb with furniture, games, boats, chariots, and beautiful silk robes. He wanted to make sure his spirit had everything for a happy afterlife.

The emperor wanted to protect his spirit from tomb robbers. First he had the giant tomb hidden under a man-made hill. Then, a mile from the tomb, he ordered thousands of workers to make an army of

Emperor 's Tomb

clay soldiers. The emperor believed that once this army was buried, the soldiers would magically come alive. They would protect the emperor from enemies forever and ever.

Pits with Terra-Cotta Soldiers

Chapter Three
Building a Clay Army

From every part of the empire,
hundreds of craftsmen came and set up
workshops near the emperor's tomb.

They used clay from nearby Mount Li. It took more than ten years to make the soldiers. (It is believed there are about 8,000 soldiers in all.) The army was finished by the time the emperor died in 210 BC.

The clay soldiers, wooden chariots, and clay horses were placed in three pits close to one another. A fourth pit has also been found, but it was empty.

The largest pit (Pit 1) is longer than two football fields. It contains the main forces of the army, about 6,000 foot soldiers.

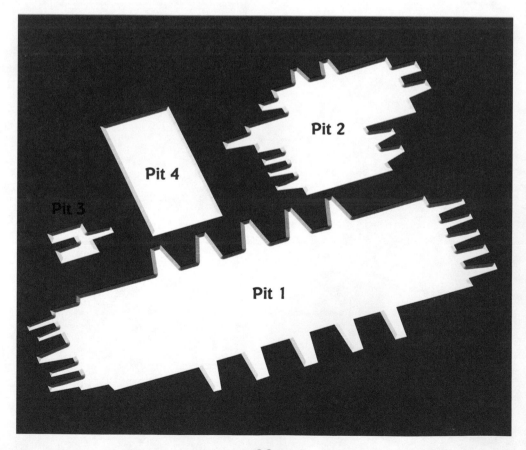

Pit 2 is much smaller and is filled with charioteers and their teams of horses. The cavalry troops would have backed up the foot soldiers from Pit 1. The clay horses are Mongolian ponies—not very big, but very strong. Their manes were trimmed short so they wouldn't get caught in their harnesses.

Archaeologists believe that the charioteers may have once stood in real wooden chariots. You can see that the charioteers' hands look as if they are holding reins.

In 1980, two bronze chariots were found not far from the clay army. The chariots are only half the size of real ones, but, in every other way, the one in the photo below is exactly what a war chariot would have looked like.

Pit 3 is the smallest. It contains about 70 soldiers. Archaeologists think that Pit 3 represents army headquarters. The officers are in a U-shaped group as if discussing plans for the next battle.

Today the pits are open to the public.
Visitors can watch groups of workers as they
uncover more figures.

Of course, the emperor of Qin never meant for anyone to see his army. After the soldiers were placed in the pits, they were covered with a wooden roof. Ten feet of dirt was shoveled on top of them so no one could tell what lay underground.

For 2,200 years, the thousands of clay soldiers remained a secret. Then, in 1974, those modern-day farmers came to dig a well, and the whole world found out about a true wonder of the ancient world!

Chapter Four

Works of Art

From a distance, the gray soldiers look the same: like a giant-sized toy army. Yet each soldier is clearly an individual.

Amazingly, no two soldiers are alike.
Their faces are different. Some are old;
some are young. Some look tired; some look
like they can't wait for the battle to start.

Their hairstyles are also different. In ancient times Chinese men wore their long hair in fancy buns and topknots.

Their uniforms are different. The uniforms are exact copies of what real soldiers wore. The archers and foot soldiers were the lowest-ranking soldiers, so they have the plainest uniforms.

The generals, of course, wore the most elegant uniforms. Some of their caps had feathers. Sometimes their shoes turned up at the toes. Their armor was patterned in small iron rings that look like fish scales.

Here you see a computer image of a clay general. It shows how he must have looked when he had just been made. Every single soldier in the emperor's army was painted with bright colors. So were the horses. Now most of the soldiers have only tiny traces of paint left.

Once in a while a soldier is found that still has bright paint in places. But when it's dug out, most of the paint curls and peels off.

Scientists are trying to create a special varnish to brush over painted figures to hold the paint in place.

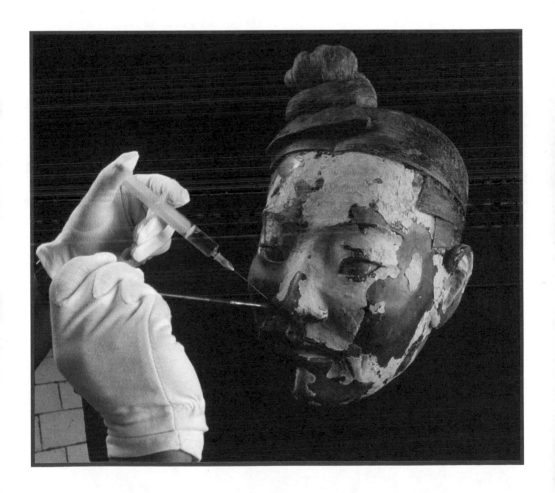

Today, craftsmen near the pits make copies of the soldiers. This helps archaeologists learn more about how the original army was made. Modern craftsmen have much better kilns than those used in ancient times. (Kilns are ovens that bake clay until it hardens.) Yet no copies ever come out as hard or shiny as the originals. Why? Nobody knows—it is a mystery.

An even bigger mystery is what lies inside the emperor's tomb. Nobody knows the answer because the tomb has never been opened. Nor does the Chinese government plan to do so anytime soon. Work will not start until archaeologists are sure the tomb can be opened without damaging any of the treasures inside.

As for the emperor's body, according to historical records, it rests in a heavy, bronze coffin.

Like the ancient Egyptians, the Chinese believed a dead person's body needed to be preserved as a "home" for the soul.

In ancient times the custom was to dress the body of someone important in a

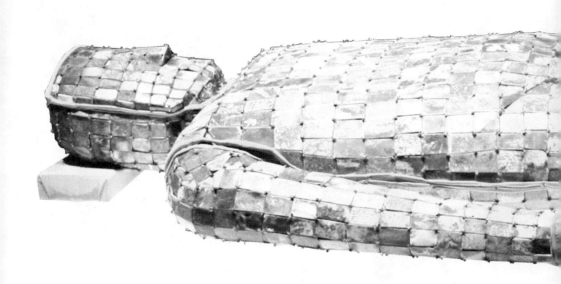

suit made from hundreds of pieces of thin jade. Jade was considered more precious than gold. It was also supposed to have the power to keep a dead body from decaying.

The first emperor died when he was 49 years old. Three years after his death, peasants rose up against the empire. One of their leaders started a new royal family.

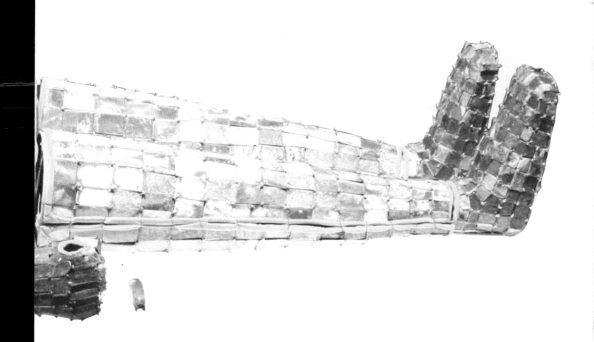

Yet now millions of people come to the first emperor's burial place. They visit the covered pits to see the clay soldiers. So in some way the emperor of Qin got his wish—he lives on in the memory of all who see his amazing hidden army.

Picture Readers

BENNY'S BIG BUBBLE
THE BIG SNOWBALL
CALLING ALL CATS
DOG WASH DAY
DON'T WAKE THE BABY!
IN A DARK, DARK HOUSE
IS THAT YOU, SANTA?
LOTS OF HEARTS
OTTO THE CAT
PICKY NICKY
PIG OUT!
SILLY WILLY
SPACE KID
TOO NOISY!

Station Stop 1: Beginning to Read

APPLES AND HOW THEY GROW
BAD HAIR DAY
BEST FRIENDS
BOSS FOR A DAY
THE BRAVEST CAT!
BUSY BUGS
BUTTERFLIES
CAT SHOW
COWBOY ROY
DOLL PARTY
DOUBLE-HEADER
THE FLYING HORSE
FROGS
THE GINGERBREAD KID GOES TO SCHOOL
HIDE-AND-SEEK ALL WEEK
ICE-COLD BIRTHDAY
JOHNNY APPLESEED
KATE SKATES
KIT AND KAT
LEMONADE STAND
LOOK! I CAN READ!
LOOK! I CAN TIE MY SHOES!
LUCKY GOES TO SCHOOL!
ME AND MY ROBOT
ME AND MY ROBOT #2: THE SHOW-AND-TELL SHOW-OFF
MEET TROUBLE
MONKEY SEE, MONKEY DO
NINA, NINA BALLERINA
NINA, NINA, AND THE COPYCAT BALLERINA
NINA, NINA, STAR BALLERINA
PAJAMA PARTY
PAL AND SAL
PAL THE PONY
PRINCESS BUTTERCUP
PRINCESS FOR A DAY
SHAPE SPOTTERS
SHARKS!
SNAIL CITY
SNUG BUG
SPIDER'S LUNCH
SPLAT!
STARS
THAT BAD, BAD CAT!
T-REX IS MISSING!
TURTLES
WATER
WHAT A HUNGRY PUPPY!
WHO STOLE THE COOKIES?

Station Stop 2: Reading with Help

100 MONSTERS IN MY SCHOOL
AMAZING ARCTIC ANIMALS
BABY ALLIGATOR
BABY ELEPHANT
BABY MEERKATS
BABY OTTER
A BABY PANDA IS BORN
BABY WOLF
BATS: CREATURES OF THE NIGHT
BEAR CUB
BENNY THE BIG SHOT GOES TO CAMP
BIG CATS
BLACK OUT!
BUG OUT!
CAVEMAN MANNERS AND OTHER POLITE POEMS
CHEETAH CUBS
CLUB PET AND OTHER FUNNY POEMS
CORAL REEFS
DEAR TOOTH FAIRY
DINOSAUR EGGS
DO DOLPHINS REALLY SMILE?
EARTHQUAKES
EEK! STORIES TO MAKE YOU SHRIEK
EGYPTIAN GODS AND GODDESSES
EMPEROR PENGUINS
FAKE OUT!
FAR OUT!
FIREFLIES
FLAMINGOS
FLIGHT OF THE BUTTERFLIES
FLOWER GIRL
FREAK OUT!
GIANT LIZARDS
GIANT SQUID
GORILLAS
GRAPHS
GRASSHOPPER PIE AND OTHER POEMS
GROSS OUT!
HELLO, TWO-WHEELER!
HONEYBEES
I BROUGHT MY RAT FOR SHOW-AND-TELL
I'VE GOT THE BACK-TO-SCHOOL BLUES
JACKIE ROBINSON: HE LED THE WAY
KNIGHTS
MARTIN LUTHER KING, JR. AND THE MARCH ON WASHINGTON
MAXED OUT!
THE MIRACLE OF EASTER
THE MONSTER MALL
MUMMIES
MY SOCCER MOM FROM MARS
NIGHT FLIGHT: CHARLES LINDBERGH'S INCREDIBLE ADVENTURE
NO ROOM AT THE INN
PINK SNOW
PIRATE SCHOOL
PLANETS
POLAR BEARS
PONIES
PRINCESS LULU GOES TO CAMP
RED, WHITE, AND BLUE
SACAJAWEA
SITTING BULL
SNAKES
UNO
VOLCANOES
WAGON TRAIN
WAY DOWN DEEP
WHALES
YOU CAN'T SMELL A FLOWER WITH YOUR EAR!

Station Stop 3: Reading Alone

ALICE IN WONDERLAND
AMISTAD: THE STORY OF A SLAVE SHIP
ANNE OF GREEN GABLES
BLACK BEAUTY
THE BOWWOW BAKE SALE
BREAKFAST AT DANNY'S DINER
CIVIL WAR SUB: THE MYSTERY OF THE *HUNLEY*
DAVID BECKHAM: BORN TO PLAY
DEREK JETER: A YANKEE HERO
A DOLL NAMED DORA ANNE
GEORGE WASHINGTON'S MOTHER
GO, FRACTIONS!
GOOFBALL MALONE ACE DETECTIVE: FOLLOW THAT FLEA!
GOOFBALL MALONE ACE DETECTIVE: SMELL THAT CLUE!
HOCKEY HOTSHOTS
HOOP STARS
HURRICANES
A HORSE NAMED SEABISCUIT
ICKSTORY: MUMMIES
ICKSTORY: VAMPIRES
JUST A FEW WORDS, MR. LINCOLN
LANCE ARMSTRONG: THE RACE OF HIS LIFE
LEBRON JAMES: KING OF THE COURT
LIGHTNING: IT'S ELECTRIFYING
A LITTLE PRINCESS
MAGNETS
MARS: THE RED PLANET
THE *MONITOR*: THE IRON WARSHIP THAT CHANGED THE WORLD
THE MYSTERIES OF THE BERMUDA TRIANGLE
PARDON THAT TURKEY
POCAHONTAS
RACE CAR DRIVERS: START YOUR ENGINES!
SAMMY SOSA: HE'S THE MAN
SARAH HUGHES: GOLDEN GIRL
THE SECRET GARDEN
SHAQUILLE O'NEAL
STOCK CAR KINGS
STORM CHASERS
TERROR BELOW! TRUE SHARK STORIES
TIGER WOODS
TONY HAWK AND ANDY MACDONALD: RIDE TO THE TOP
TRUE BLUE
UNDERCOVER KID: TUNA SURPRISE

HIDDEN ARMY
Clay Soldiers of Ancient China

One day in 1974, farmers in China were digging a well. Suddenly they found something. Was it a rock? No. It was a part of a life-size clay soldier. There was a whole army of clay soldiers buried right below the farmers' feet! Who made the clay army and why? Find out in this exciting true story about the first emperor of China.

Station Stop 1	Station Stop 2	Station Stop 3
Beginning to Read	**Reading with Help**	**Reading Alone**
✦ Simple words	✦ Short sentences	✦ Longer text
✦ Big type	✦ Simple plots	✦ Harder words
✦ Picture clues	✦ Simple dialogue	✦ More complex stories
✦ Word repetition		

The books in this series are listed inside. Read them all!

$3.99 US
($4.99 CAN)

GROSSET & DUNLAP
www.penguin.com/youngreaders

ISBN 978-0-448-45580-8

EAN

9 780448 455808

50399>